D1559926

JUST STAND UP

A TRIBUTE TO BLACK COMEDIANS

ERIC REESE

CONTENTS

INTRODUCTION

There has been humor in the United States for as long as it has been a country. After all, life was tough and laughing was one important way to cope and survive. However, standup comedy as an art form took a while to evolve and catch on. The history is rich and many books have been written on the subject. This article will serve as a very annotated version so that the reader can use it for a "jumping off place" to study more deeply those parts that are of interest.

One of the first types of organized standup comedy in the United States was the minstrel show that came on the scene in the early 1800s. It was sometimes referred to as "black face comedy". Although appalling by 21st century standards, this brand of comedy was widely popular when it started. The all white casts would paint their faces black and begin using the stereotypical mannerisms of the blacks for their material. It has always been said that comedy reflects the times. And like it or not, this was the state of the country in the 1800s. The minstrel show remained popular through to the mid-19th century and began to loose favor as the United States views on racism and slavery began to change.

As the minstrel show's popularity waned, vaudeville began to be a popular form or standup or pre-standup comedy. In addition to comedy, vaudeville acts included dancers, magicians and actors. Some shows even included clown-like acts. Just a few of the main comedians of this brand of comedy are - Fred DuPres, George Burns and Gracie Allen, Groucho Marx and the Marx Brothers and Ezera kendall. Vaudeville comedians relied less on the spoken word for laughs and instead used, props and physical comedy. This is because they did not have microphones and instead had to rely on the physical type of comedy.

This was the beginning of "comedy for the masses". But while this was very good news for the general public, it came with a price for the performers. They could no longer rely on the physical aspect of their comedy, they now only had their material and timing to get their audiences to laugh. Some comedians were able to make the transition from Vaudeville to more of a spoken word type of comedy. Some of the notable comedians that made this transition are: Jack Benny, Bob Hope, Milton Berle and George Burns.

The addition of the radio was not the only development that was groundbreaking for standup comedy. The microphone was also available for the comedian to apply their craft. And again, the comedians from Vaudeville had to adjust their shows to more spoken word comedy than physical comedy.

Now, comedians were able to perform standup comedy as we now know it. It is at this point in the history that they changes in standup comedy is more content related instead of the physical way that it is performed. Standup comedy throughout the following decades was a reflection of the what events were happening at the time and also the morality and accepted subjects in the country during those decade.

JACKIE "MOMS" MABLEY

Jackie "Moms" Mabley was born in Brevard, North Carolina and rose to national recognition as a standup comedian in the early 1960s. A pioneer of social satire, she has strongly influenced such contemporary Black comedians as Richard Pryor and Whoopi Goldberg. Mabley was also known for her compassion and kindness; these qualities earned her the endearing sobriquet "Moms". Born Loretta Mary Aiken, Mabley grew up in a large family in the south. Her father ran several businesses while her mother presided over a large household that included boarders.

When Loretta was 11, her father died when his fire truck overturned and exploded. Encouraged by her grandmother to make a life for herself, she departed for Cleveland, Ohio. After singing and dancing in local shows, she began performing throughout the country. Traveling the vaudeville circuit, she experienced overt racism and demeaning working conditions and deflected her pain through satirical wit that drew heavily from black folk traditions. Mabley's career took off when, in 1921, the husband-wife vaudeville team, Butterbeans and Susie, invited her to perform with them in Pittsburgh, Pennsylvania.

In her comedy routines, Mabley adopted a stage persona based loosely on her own grandmother but with a distinctly cantankerous and sassy edge. She was known for her folksy humor and ribald jokes and affectionately referred to her audience as her "children." Onstage Mabley became famous for her gaudy housedresses, floppy hats, and oversized clodhoppers. During the 1960s, she recorded more than 20 albums of her comedy routines and appeared on television shows hosted by Harry Belafonte, Mike Douglas, Merv Griffin, and Bill Cosby.

At a Glance...

Born Loretta Mary Aiken, March 19,1894 or 1897, in Brevard, North Carolina; died May 23, 1975 in White Plains, New York. Children: a daughter, Bonnie, and one adopted son.

Awards: Gold Record for The Funniest Woman in the World, 1960.

Comedienne. Began performing in the Theatre Owners Booking Association (TOBA), circa 1915; changed name to Jackie Mabley, circa 1920; discovered by Butter-beans and Susie in Dallas and signed to a talent agent, 1921 ; first played in the Harlem Renaissance theaters of New York, 1923; appeared in the musicals Miss Bandana, 1927 and Fast and Furious, 1931 ; appeared in the films Emperor Jones, 1933, Big Timers, 1945, Killer Dilier, 1948, Boarding House Blues, 1948, and Amazing Grace, 1974; albums for Chess Records include, The Funniest Woman in the World; At the UN; At the Playboy Club; At the Geneva Conference; Breaks It Up; Young Men, Si; IGot Something to Tell You; Funny Sides; Moms Wows; Best of Moms Mabley; Man in My Life; Moms Breaks Up the Network; Sings; albums for Mercury Records include Out on a Limb; Mom the Word; At the White House; Her Young Thing; Now Hear This; Best of Moms; Abraham, Martin, and John; Live at Sing Sing; I Like 'Em Young; first appearance on television, A Time for Laughter, 1967; subsequent appearances on the Flip Wilson Show, the Bill Cosby Show, the Smothers Brothers show, the Ed Sullivan show; appeared on Grammy Award show, 1973; play on Mabley's life, Moms, written by Ben Caldwell and featuring Clarice Taylor opened, 1986.

Hardships growing up and making it out

By age 14, Loretta had been raped twice at age 11, by an elderly black man, and age 13, by a white sheriff. Both rapes resulted in pregnancies and the children were given away for adoption. More hardship followed when Mabley's father, who was also a volunteer fireman, was killed when a fire engine exploded and her mother was run over by a truck while returning home from church on Christmas Day. Although it is unclear whether Mabley was ever forced to marry a man against her will, arranged marriage became a staple of her comedy act. "My daddy liked him so I had to marry that old man," she'd say. "He was the nearest to death you've ever seen in your life. His shadow weighed more than he did. He got out of breath threading a needle. And ugleeee! He was so ugly he hurt my feelings...He was so weak, when we got married somebody threw one grain of rice and it knocked him out."

At the age of fourteen, Mabley left North Carolina to seek her fortune as an entertainer. "I was pretty and didn't want to become a prostitute," she's quoted as saying in Funny Women, about her decision to go into show business. She could sing, dance, and tell a joke, which made her popular on the black vaudeville circuit, the Theatre Owners Booking Association (TOBA), which toured the South in the tradition of the pre-Civil War minstrel shows. Although Mabley was a capable singer and dancer, her primary strength was comedy and she would often appear in skits with other performers. While performing on the TOBA circuit, she met Jack Mabley, another entertainer who became her boyfriend. After a brief relationship, she took his name and began to perform as Jackie Mabley. "Jack was my first boyfriend," Mabley recalled to Ebony in 1974. "I was real uptight with him and he certainly was real uptight with me; you'd better believe. He took a lot off me and the least I could do was take his name."

While performing in Dallas one night in 1921, Mabley was spotted by the song and dance team of Butterbeans and Susie, an act noted for risque comedy songs like "I Want a Hot Dog for My Roll." They told me I was too good for the place I was in," she recalled to Ebony,"and they said they would send me to an agent who would get me more money and some better book-

4

ings." Mabley signed with the agent and became a regular on the "Chitlin Circuit," a string of urban ghetto moviehouses and theaters, and was making upwards of $90 a week compared to the $14 a week she'd been pulling in with TOBA. By 1923, Mabley had traveled to New York where she began performing in famous Harlem Renaissance theaters like Connie's Inn and the Cotton Club and often shared the stage with legendary performers like Louis Armstrong, Count Basie, Duke Ellington, and Cab Calloway.

The Birth of "Moms"

While still in her twenties and performing on the TOBA circuit, Mabley began to develop the stage persona of a wise old woman who wore the flappy clothes that later became her trademark. "I had in my mind a woman about 60 or 65, even, when I first came up," Mabley recalled to Mark Jacobson of New York,"she's a good woman, with an eye for shady dealings...she was like my granny, the most beautiful woman I ever knew. She was the one who convinced me to go make something of myself...she was so gentle, but she kept her children in line, best believe that." Mabley had earned the nickname "Moms" because of her tendency to "mother" her fellow performers, and she adopted this nickname for her character. In addition to her comedic stage performances as "Moms," Mabley also performed in musical-comedies such as Miss Bandana in 1927, Fast and Furious in 1931 which featured the writer Zora Neale Hurston, as well as small, race movies including Paul Robeson's Emperor Jones in 1933.

In 1939 Mabley became the first female comedian to perform at Harlem's Apollo Theater, a major venue for black performers. Mabley soon became a regular at the Apollo and would often play for fifteen-week stints, changing her act each week. She also contributed to the writing of comedy shows at the Apollo as well as writing her own act with the help of her younger brother, Eddie Parton. She quickly became a favorite with the Apollo audiences, who began laughing as soon as she walked on the stage. By the 1950s, Mabley had become a popular attraction in black nightclubs around the country. "In thirty-five minutes on stage," she's quoted as saying in Funny Women, "I can keep laughter in a certain range, building higher and higher 'til when I tell the last joke, they're all laughing like mad." Despite her popularity with blackaudiences, however, mainstream success with white audiences still eluded her.

While her qquest for a young man was a pervasive part of her act, Mabley also began to incorporate absurd tales from her "life" such as hanging out on the White House lawn with President Eisenhower, Adam Clayton Powell, Bo Diddley, and Big Maybelle. Or the advice she used to give to then First Lady, Mamie Eisenhower: "I said, 'Listen, Mame.' And she said, "Yes, Mrs. Mabley.'" Because she incorporated race related stories in her act, Mabley is considered one of the pioneers of social satire. Mel Watkins, author of On the Real Side, a history of black humor, noted that Mabley "foreshadowed the shift to direct social commentary and stand-up techniques that would define humor by the late fifties." Typical of these race related tales was the story Mabley would tell of driving in the South: "I was on my way down to Miami... I mean They-ami. I was ridin' along in my Cadillac, you know, goin' through one of them little towns in South Carolina. Pass through a red light. One of them big cops come runnin' over to me, say, "Hey woman, don't you know you went through a red light?' I say, "Yeah I know I went through a red light.' "Well, what did you do that for?' I said, 'Cause I seen all you white folks goin' on the green light...I thought the red light was for us!'"

Finally came the success ...

In the late 1950s, comedy records became wildly popular and record companies were actively looking to cash in on the trend. Chess Records, home of blues greats Muddy Waters and Howlin Wolf and rock and roll legends Chuck Berry and Bo Diddley, approached Mabley about recording a comedy album. After some hesitation, Mabley signed on with Chess in 1960 and recorded The Funniest Woman Alive before a live audience in Chicago. The record went on to sell over one million copies and earned Mabley a gold record. In 1966, Mabley recorded Now Hear This for the Mercury label, an album so full of raunchy tales and blue humor that it became a hit at stag parties. Mabley's raw humor is often cited as a reason for her lack of television appearances, a topic she addresses in Watkins's book. "It's you and others in your position," she explained to a group of television executives, "who keep me working where I have to use that kind of material."

Mabley first appeared on television in 1967 on "A Time for Laughter", an all-black comedy show produced by Harry Belafonte. Other spots followed on the Flip Wilson Show, the

Smothers Brothers Show, as well as shows hosted by Mike Douglas and Bill Cosby. By the late 1960s, Mabley's television appearances and hit comedy records had made her a bona fide star. Her salary at the Apollo increased from $1,000 a week in 1961 to a $10,000 a week headline spot in 1968. After nearly fifty years in show business, Mabley was an overnight success.

In 1974, Mabley starred in Amazing Grace, the story of an honest woman who tries to reform a corrupt black politician. Playing the title role of Grace Teasdale Grimes, it was Mabley's first movie project since her small roles in the race films of the thirties and forties. "It sho' wasn't because I didn't have the talent, "she told Ebony about the dearth of movie roles for her. "I can do almost anything connected with show business. I was taught to do everything." During the filming of Amazing Grace, Mabley suffered a serious heart attack. She had a pacemaker installed and returned to the set three weeks later to complete the film. The film opened to mixed reviews, but did well enough at the box office to be considered a success for Mabley. Unfortunately, success came only at the end of her career. "I try not to be bitter," she confessed to Jacobson. "I would have liked to have gotten my chance earlier, but that's the way things were in those days...better times are coming."

Following the release of Amazing Grace, Mabley's health took a turn for the worse and she died on May 23, 1975. "Had she been white," comedian Dick Gregory said at her funeral, "she'd have been known fifty years ago." Although Mabley enjoyed mainstream success only for a brief time, she still occupies an important place in the history of American comedy. A social and show business pioneer, Mabley worked hard, persevered despite many obstacles, and made the road to success easier for future black performers. "I just tell folks the truth," she's quoted as saying in Funny Women."If they don't want the truth, then don't come to Moms. Anybody that comes to me, I'll help 'em. I don't say anything I don't mean."

REDD FOXX

Redd Foxx was a pioneering standup comic, recording artist, and comedic actor. He is best known for playing the character Fred G. Sanford on Sanford and Son, one of the most popular television series in the 1970s.

Early Years and Education

Jon Elroy Sanford was born in St. Louis, Missouri, on December 9, 1922, to Fred Glenn Sanford and Mary Alma Hughes Sanford. After Jon's father abandoned the family, Mary moved to Chicago to look for work, leaving Jon and his older brother, Fred G. Sanford Jr., with their grandmother.

DuSable High School

The boys eventually joined their mother in Chicago, where Jon finished middle school at Carter School and then attended DuSable High School. There he and some classmates formed a band called the Four Bon Bons. Jon dropped out of school at age sixteen and moved with the band to Harlem in New York City.

From Coast to Coast

Jon's band (now the Jump Swinging Six) performed on a national radio show, but soon broke up. In Harlem, Jon was nicknamed "Foxy," because he was a sharply dressed ladies' man. He washed dishes at the same restaurant that employed the great jazz musician Charlie Parker. There he befriended Malcolm Little, who later became the civil rights leader known as Malcolm X. Jon and Malcolm, who were nicknamed "Chicago Red" and "Detroit Red," spent their evenings doing drugs, chasing women, and committing petty crimes.

In 1945, Jon became an emcee at a club in Baltimore, Maryland. His new stage name, "Redd Foxx," was a combination of his two nicknames, spelled with double consonants like the famous baseball player, Jimmie Foxx. Redd was approached to record a set of comedy albums in Newark, New Jersey, where he met and married Evelyn Killibrew. The records flopped, but Redd formed an act called "Foxx and White" with fellow comedian, Slappy White. They found success touring the national Chitlin' Circuit in the late 1940s and early 1950s. After moving to Los Angeles in 1952 to open for singer Dinah Washington, their act (and Redd's marriage) broke up.

. . .

King of the Party Records

In Los Angeles, Redd became an assistant to the radio DJ Johnny Otis and acted on Otis's local television show. He also started doing standup comedy as a solo act. Due to segregation, Redd could not perform in the "mainstream" clubs frequented by whites, but this allowed him to experiment with edgier material without fear of being arrested for breaking obscenity laws. His raunchy new act became popular in Los Angeles's black clubs. In 1955, Foxx married singer Betty Jeanne Harris and recorded a hit comedy album, Laff of the Party.

Redd's recording success helped his standup career flourish. By the early 1960s he was performing at large integrated clubs in Las Vegas and had homes in that city, Los Angeles, and St. Louis. In 1964 he appeared on the Today Show (with a censored act), then performed on several other nationally televised shows, including The Tonight Show with Johnny Carson.

Sanford and Son

In 1970, Redd played the part of a wily junkyard owner in the film Cotton Comes to Harlem. This led to a similar role on an American remake of the British sitcom, Steptoe and Son. Redd named his character Fred G. Sanford, after his brother, who died at the age of forty-six. The character's son, Lamont, was named after Lamont Ousley, Redd's bandmate in the Four Bon Bons. The show was renamed Sanford and Son. Although Sanford's age was given as sixty-five and Redd was only forty-eight, Foxx's hard-partying lifestyle aged him enough to look the part. The character was based in part on Redd's mother, Mary, who often faked illnesses to get attention.

Sanford and Son debuted on NBC on January 14, 1972. Redd's standup comedy experience allowed him to improvise before the live studio audience to hilarious results, especially when he was performing one of Sanford's signature fake heart attacks. Foxx won a Golden Globe for his portrayal of Sanford, and Sanford and Son finished the season as the sixth-highest-rated show on television.

Sanford and Son was groundbreaking not only for its humor, but also as a showcase for lesser-known African American performers. The show was second in the ratings by the end of its second season. Foxx signed a lucrative contract and became a popular advertising spokesman; however, before the end of the third season, he left the show over a contract dispute. He held out into the fourth season and was awarded a new contract that was tied for the richest salary on television. After his divorce from Betty in 1976, Foxx married Korean immigrant Yun Chi Chung (called Joi) and starred in another movie, "Norman, Is That You?"

A Falling Star

Redd performed on Sanford and Son until 1977. He then signed the richest contract in television to star in a variety show on ABC called The Redd Foxx Comedy Hour. After initially gaining high ratings, the show was canceled at the end of its first season. Foxx returned to his standup career in Las Vegas, but was involved in a number of lawsuits ranging from a contract dispute with ABC to charges that he had harassed a waitress and assaulted one of his employees.

For Redd, the 1980s were characterized by massive debt, business failures, and another divorce. He filed for bankruptcy in 1983. In 1986, The Redd Foxx Show debuted, but it only lasted a few months. A Broadway show, Redd Foxx and Friends, failed the next year. In 1989 the IRS raided Redd's home and confiscated almost everything in an attempt to recover enough to pay his back taxes.

That same year, Redd starred in the movie Harlem Nights with Eddie Murphy. Murphy was so impressed by Foxx's chemistry with Della Reese (Redd's longtime friend from the Chitlin' Circuit) that he created a new sitcom for the pair in 1991. Shortly after his fourth marriage to Ka Ho Cho, Foxx's new show, The Royal Family, debuted to high ratings. Unfortunately, Foxx's marriage and career comeback were cut short by a stroke of fate.

Death and Legacy

"Redd said, 'Ah, give me a break' and reached for the chair and did what we thought was a pratfall, 'cause he did that all the time. And we all stood there laughing while he was laying on the floor. He'd had a heart attack." — Della Reese.

Redd's years of hard living finally caught up with him on October 11, 1991, when he collapsed on the set of The Royal Family. Initially, his costars thought he was performing one of his famous fake heart attacks. Foxx died of heart failure at a hospital later that evening at the age of sixty-eight. At the time of his death, he still owed millions to the IRS.

Although Redd Foxx is mainly remembered for his iconic character Fred G. Sanford, his career made many lasting impressions on American comedy. Foxx was one of the first black comedians to find mainstream success, and his uncensored style helped pave the way for other comics who used racy material. The success of Sanford and Son inspired several other sitcoms with primarily African American casts, and Redd used the show as a national stage to promote black performers. Foxx helped launch the careers of several black comedians, such as Richard Pryor and Bernie Mac, and has been named as a major influence by many others, such as Eddie Murphy, Chris Rock, and Jamie Foxx (who adopted his last name). Redd Foxx is honored on the St. Louis Walk of Fame and the historic Apollo Theater's Walk of Fame.

NIPSEY RUSSELL

Nipsey Russell was a comedian who appeared as a guest panelist on several game shows throughout the 1960s, '70s, '80s and '90s. Russell also played a leading role in the 1978 film, "The Wiz" as the Tin Man. His comedic routines were landmark in that he refused to use stereotypical dialects or play stereotypical roles in his acts. His work as a comedian who defied stereotypes broke barriers for rising comedians of all backgrounds. He died on October 2, 2005.

Early Life

Nipsey Russell was born as Julius Russell on what was believed to be October 13, 1924, in Atlanta, Georgia. Because his birth certificate has been lost, his precise birth date remains unknown, but upon his death in 2005 friends said that he was 80 years old. Russell received the nickname "Nipsey" as a baby

—"My mother just liked the way the name Nipsey sounded," he explained. Russell began performing when he was only a toddler, and at the age of 3 he joined a children's dance team called "The Ragamuffins of Rhythm."

By the age of 6, he had become the singing and dancing master of ceremonies for a local Atlanta children's troupe run by the jazz musician Eddie Heywood, Sr. Russell traced his interest in comedy back to seeing a performance by the African-American performer Jack Wiggins around the age of 9. Russell recalled, "He came out immaculately attired in a well-dressed street suit and he tap-danced. As he danced, he told little jokes in between. He was so clean in his language and was lacking in any drawl, he just inspired me. I wanted to do that."

In addition to his knack for performing, the young Russell was also a precocious scholar with literary inclinations. By age 10, he was devouring the works of English poets such as Chaucer, Shelley and Keats as well as working through Homer's epics in the original Greek. He graduated early from high school at the age of 15, having spent his senior year living with an aunt in Cincinnati so that he could attend the University of Cincinnati tuition-free. However, Russell's studies were interrupted by the outbreak of World War II. He served a four-year enlistment in the Army and was commissioned as a captain in the field. Upon the conclusion of the war, he returned to the University of Cincinnati and graduated with a degree in classical literature in 1946.

Comedic Career

After graduating from college, Russell decided to forgo academic pursuits to try his luck as a standup comedian. At the time Russell embarked on his show business career in the late 1940s and early 1950s, the United States remained deeply segregated, and he performed in exclusively black comedy clubs on the East Coast, in the Midwest and in Canada. However, by the late 1950s, Russell was booking shows at the top Catskills resorts as well as at the Apollo in Harlem.

Around the same time, he began a seven-year tenure—the longest in the club's history—at the Baby Grand, a Manhattan nightclub that, largely due to Russell's act, began to attract white crowds as well as black. It was at the Baby Grand that Russell refined his comedic style, an intelligent, often overtly erudite routine that dealt with a wide variety of subject matter. "I use mother-in-law jokes, kid jokes, tax jokes—anything that works," Russell explained. He defied the stereotypical roles associated with black performers by persistently refusing to use dialects or play a fool.

During the 1960s and 1970s, Russell capitalized on his success as a stage performer to become a fixture on television comedy shows. He appeared frequently on The Tonight Show, Missing Links, The Ed Sullivan Show, What's My Line and The Jackie Gleason Show. It was on Missing Links with Ed McMahon in 1964 that Russell first began incorporating into his routines the brief, rhymed poems that would become his trademark and earn him the title "The Poet Laureate of Television." A typical example of one of his humorous poems went: "Before we lose our autonomy/ And our economy crumbles into dust/ We should attack Japan, lose the war/ And let Japan take care of us."

Game shows

Russell became the first black performer to become a regular panelist on a daily network game show when he joined ABC's Missing Links in 1964. Another ABC show, Rhyme and Reason, had poetry as a premise:

Host: Conny Van Dyke looks like a girl I once dated...

Russell: And now, all my dreams are strictly X-rated!

Host: Jack said to Jill when they came down the hill...

Russell: We didn't go there for water — I hope you take the pill!

In 1971, he started as a featured panelist on To Tell the Truth, which led to his being hired for The Match Game when Goodson-Todman Productions revived it two years later. He also served as panelist in 1968 on the syndicated version of What's My Line?. Producer Bob Stewart featured him regularly as a panelist on Pyramid throughout its 1970s and 1980s runs. Russell would host two game show pilots: one was Star Words for Mark Goodson in 1983 and a revival of Jackpot for Bob Stewart in 1984. These pilots were shot for CBS, but neither pilot was picked up by the network. Russell went on to host two revivals of Jack Barry and Dan Enright's Juvenile Jury for BET from 1983 to 1984, then again for syndication from 1989 to 1991. In 1985, Russell hosted the short-lived 1985 NBC game show Your Number's Up, which was produced by Sande Stewart.

Acting Career

In addition to his comedy routines, Russell also enjoyed a successful acting career. He landed his first major acting role as police officer in the sitcom Car 54, Where Are You? and went on to roles in Barefoot in the Park (1970) and The Red Skelton Hour (1967-1968). Russel's most acclaimed acting performance came as the Tin Man in The Wiz, an all-black remake of The Wizard of Oz costarring Diana Ross, Michael Jackson and Richard Pryor. While continuing to perform live shows in New York City and Las Vegas, in his later years Russell became a staple of daytime television with long-running roles on The $20,000 Pyramid, Password Plus and Hollywood Squares.

Legacy

Nipsey Russell was never married and did not have any children. He often joked, "I have enough trouble living with myself, how could I ever live with anyone else?" Russell passed away in New York City on October 2, 2005 after a yearlong struggle with cancer.

With his beaming smile, intelligent wit and endless supply of clever rhymes, Nipsey Russell brought laughter to generations of club-goers and television-watchers, both black and white, while helping to break down the racial barriers that had long plagued the American entertainment industry. He was an entertainer who both reflected and helped bring about the increasingly multicultural makeup of American society. Extolling American diversity in characteristically humorous fashion, Russell once quipped, "America is the only place in the world where you can work in an Arab home in a Scandinavian neighborhood and find a Puerto Rican baby eating matzo balls with chopsticks."

Later career and death

During the 1990s Russell gained popularity with a new generation of television viewers as a regular on Late Night with Conan O'Brien. Russell would often appear during comedy sketches between scheduled guests and deliver his trademark rhymes.

Russell's final TV appearance was as a panelist on a game show-themed week on the final season of the Tom Bergeron version of Hollywood Sqquares.

BILL COSBY

Comedian Bill Cosby gained widespread popularity for TV shows including 'I Spy,' 'Fat Albert' and 'The Cosby Show.' In his later years, Cosby's legendary status became tarnished with numerous accusations of sexual misconduct including a recent conviction in Pennsylvania in April 2018.

He was born on July 12, 1937, in Philadelphia, Pennsylvania and later dropped out of high school to join the U.S. Navy. Later, he left college to become a stand-up comedian. Cosby's first acting assignment, in the espionage series I Spy (1965-68), made him the first black actor to co-star in a leading dramatic role on network television. He was also the first African-American performer to win an Emmy, doing so in 1966. Cosby's most successful work, The Cosby Show, appeared on NBC from 1984 to 1992, and was the highest-rated sitcom for several consecutive years. Cosby's legendary status became tarnished when numerous accusations of sexual misconduct surfaced in 2014.

He stood trial for three counts of aggravated indecent assault in June 2017, but escaped punishment when the judge declared a mistrial. In

Background and Early Career

Actor, comedian, writer and producer Bill Cosby was born William Henry Cosby Jr. on July 12, 1937, in Philadelphia, Pennsylvania. With numerous awards to his credit, Bill Cosby is one of the top names in comedy. He also helped break down racial barriers on television in the 1960s with I Spy and, later, The Cosby Show.

Cosby, the oldest of four boys, grew up in Philadelphia's Germantown neighborhood. At first, the Cosbys were able to get by, financially, but the family's money began to slip when Cosby's father, William Cosby Sr., began drinking heavily. After his father enlisted in the U.S. Navy, Cosby became like a parent to his brothers. Cosby's mother, Anna, worked cleaning houses. He and his family also ended up living in the Richard Allen Homes, a low-income housing project. At the age of 8, Cosby suffered a great loss when his brother James, the second oldest of the boys, died.

With money very tight for his family, Cosby started shining shoes and worked at a supermarket during his middle school years. Despite their hardships, Cosby's mother stressed the value of education and learning. She often read books to Bill and his brothers, including the Bible and works by Mark Twain. A gifted storyteller himself, Cosby learned early on that humor could be a way to make friends and get what he wanted. Cosby excelled at making things up. As one of his teachers once noted, "William should become either a lawyer or an actor because he lies so well."

In school, Cosby was bright but unmotivated. He liked to tell stories and jokes to his classmates more than he liked to do his schoolwork. One of his teachers encouraged him to put his performing talents to use in school plays, not in her classroom. At home, Cosby listened to a variety of radio programs and started imitating such comedians as Jerry Lewis. He also watched such television performers as Sid Caesar and Jack Benny whenever he could.

While he was more interested in sports than academics—he was active on his school's track and football teams—Cosby was placed in a high school for gifted students after scoring high on an IQ test. But Cosby failed to apply himself and ended up failing tenth grade twice. He switched to Germantown High School, but the academic issues continued. In frustration, Cosby dropped out of high school. He worked several odd jobs before joining the U.S. Navy in 1956.

During his military service, Cosby worked as a medical aide on ships, in several hospitals and at other facilities. He also joined the Navy's track team, where he excelled, especially in the high jump event. Regretting his decision to drop out of school, Cosby earned his high school equivalency diploma while in the service. After leaving the Navy, he went to Temple University via scholarship.

While at Temple, Cosby landed a job as a bartender at a coffee house. He told jokes there, and eventually landed work filling in for the house comedian from time to time at a nearby club. Cosby also performed as a warm-up act for his cousin's radio show. He found inspiration in the works of such comedians as Dick Gregory, an African-American comic who often talked about racial issues in his routines. Early in his career, Cosby discussed race in his act as well, but he eventually dropped it from his performances, choosing to focus on telling stories about more general and universal themes.

'I Spy' and 'Fat Albert'

Nearly halfway through his college career, Cosby decided to drop out to pursue a career in stand-up comedy. He started performing at a place in Greenwich Village, New York, and he toured extensively, winning over fans. In 1963, Cosby made his first appearance on Johnny Carson's Tonight Show, which helped introduce him to a national audience. (Cosby would go on to appear on the show dozens of times.) He also landed a recording contract and that same year released his first comedy album, Bill Cosby Is a Very Funny Fellow ... Right! He won a Grammy Award (Best Comedy Performance) for his next effort, 1964's I Started Out as a Child. For the remainder of the 1960s, Cosby released hit album after hit album, winning another five Grammys. He would later pick up two more for his recordings for children as part of The Electric Company TV series.

In 1965, Cosby also helped pave the way for African-American TV performers with a leading role in a TV series. Portraying Alexander Scott, he starred with Robert Culp in the espionage series I Spy. The two spies pretended to be a professional tennis player (Culp) traveling with his coach (Cosby). The show ran for three years, and Cosby received three consecutive Emmy Awards for his work.

Not long after I Spy ended, Cosby starred in his own sitcom. The Bill Cosby Show ran for two seasons, from 1969 to 1971, and featured the comedian as a gym teacher at a Los Angeles high school. A former aspiring teacher, Cosby went back to school at the University of Massachusetts at Amherst. Around the same time, he appeared on the educational children's series The Electric Company, and developed the animated series Fat Albert and the Cosby Kids, which he based on many of his childhood experiences. In 1977, Cosby received a doctorate in urban education from the university, having written his dissertation on Fat Albert. (Cosby had received the degree via nontraditional methods, with his screen work reportedly counting toward course credits.)

On the big screen, Cosby enjoyed box-office success with the 1974 comedy Uptown Saturday Night, co-starring Sidney Poitier and Harry Belafonte, with Poitier directing. Continuing to attract big audiences, he appeared opposite Poitier in two more comedy hits, Let's Do It Again and A Piece of the Action, in 1975 and 1977, respectively.

'The Cosby Show'

Once again turning to his life for inspiration, Cosby began working on a new television series. The sitcom focused on an upper-middle class African-American couple with five children. Each of the children's characters shared some traits of their real-life counterparts. Married since 1964, Cosby and his real-life wife, Camille, had four daughters and one son. (Cosby originally wanted the show to be about a driver and his plumber wife, with Camille joining producers to push for the show to be about a doctor and attorney.) In 1984, The Cosby Show debuted to favorable reviews and strong ratings.

Week after week, The Cosby Show drew audiences with its warm humor and believable situations. Cosby's character, Dr. Heathcliff Huxtable, became one of the most popular dads in television history. He also served as a parental figure to his young co-stars, including Sabrina Le Beauf, Lisa Bonet, Malcolm-Jamal Warner, Tempestt Bledsoe and Keshia Knight Pulliam, as well as Raven-Symoné and Erika Alexander, on set. Phylicia Rashad co-starred with Cosby as his wife, Clair. After being the highest-rated sitcom on TV for several years, the show finally ended its run in 1992.

Over the show's eight-season run, Cosby found time for other projects: He appeared in several films, including Leonard Part 6 (1987) and Ghost Dad (1990). In 1986, Cosby achieved another career milestone—becoming a bestselling author. His reflections on parenting were included in the book Fatherhood, which sold millions of copies. His opus on aging, Time Flies (1987), also enjoyed huge sales. In addition, Cosby enjoyed great popularity as a pitchman, appearing in commercials for such products as JELL-O, for which he had served as a spokesman since 1974.

After The Cosby Show, Cosby continued to work in television.

He starred in The Cosby Mysteries, in which he played a retired criminologist who sometimes helped out a detective friend. Then in 1996, he returned to sitcoms with Cosby, re-teaming with former co-star Rashad. They were unable to obtain the same level of success as their earlier effort, but they did enjoy some popularity, staying on the air for four years.

Personal Loss

While working on Cosby, the comedian experienced a deep personal loss. His only son, Ennis, was killed in 1997, shot to death while changing a tire on his car on the side of a California highway. Around the same time, Cosby was caught up in a paternity scandal. A young woman named Autumn Jackson claimed that Cosby was her father and tried to blackmail him for $40 million, saying that she would go to the tabloids if she didn't get the money. She was arrested and convicted of extortion, receiving a 26-month prison sentence. (The conviction was later overturned and then reinstated.) Cosby admitted that he had a brief encounter with Jackson's mother, but he claimed he was not Autumn's father.

While coping with these difficult episodes, Cosby took on new professional challenges. He started a series of children's picture books featuring a character named Little Bill in 1997, which also became a children's TV program. A frequent speaker at commencement ceremonies, Cosby shared his advice in 1999's Congratulations! Now What?: A Book for Graduates. He took a serious look at the education system in 2000's American Schools: The $100 Billion Challenge, and paired up with his daughter Erika for 2003's Friends of a Feather: One of Life's Little Fables.

Awards and Return to TV

Cosby has received numerous accolades for his work, including multiple Emmy, Grammy, NAACP and People's Choice awards. He was also honored with the 2002 Presidential Medal of Freedom, the 2003 Bob Hope Humanitarian Award and the 2009 Mark Twain Prize for American Humor.

In November 2013, Bill Cosby returned to the small screen with a new special on Comedy Central, Far From Finished. Directed by Robert Townsend, the production marked the comedian's first concert special in three decades.

Many Accusations of Sexual Misconduct

Cosby made headlines in 2014, not for his comedy, but his alleged misconduct. Over the years, he had faced numerous accusations of sexual assault. Cosby did not have criminal charges filed against him, but he did settle with one of his accusers out of court in 2006 after she launched a civil suit. In 2014, comedian Hannibal Buress brought new attention to earlier allegations by stating that Cosby "raped women" in his routine, according to Vulture.com.

After this incident, Cosby remained silent about these claims. More women soon came forth to claim that the comedian attacked them as well, including model Janice Dickinson. She told Entertainment Tonight that Cosby gave her wine and some type of pill before he allegedly raped her. These accusations led both NBC and Netflix to announce that they were dropping projects that they had with Cosby, with cancellations to come as well for his 2015 stand-up tour. Cosby did not respond directly to the claims. After a National Public Radio interview with Cosby in November 2014, a lawyer said in a statement that the comedian "won't dignify these allegations with any response."

That December, as more accusations of sexual assault surfaced, Cosby spoke to a reporter about the news coverage of the controversy surrounding him. He said that "I only expect the black media to uphold the standards of excellence in journalism and when you do that you have to go in with a neutral mind," according to the New York Post.

Cosby's wife Camille stood by the comedian as well, issuing a statement in December as well where she positioned her husband as "kind" and "generous" and questioned the media's publishing of accounts from women whose backgrounds hadn't been vetted. Yet in 2015 more women came forth with charges of sexual assault, with there being ultimately dozens of other accusers with allegations of misconduct. Several women, including Dickinson, also filed defamation lawsuits against Cosby.

Then in early July 2015, court documents from 2005 were allowed to be unsealed by a federal judge after an Associated Press request. Testimony from a civil suit issued by Andrea Constand revealed that Cosby had gotten hold of prescription quaaludes during the 1970s with the intention of giving the drugs to women before engaging in sexual activity. During the testimony, due to his attorney's objection, Cosby did not state whether he gave women the drugs without their knowledge. In light of the new information, the comedian did not immediately issue a public statement. Later in the month, The New York Times reported on a related deposition in which Cosby spoke of meetings with a variety of women, admitting to giving drugs as part of his interactions and sexual pursuits.

In late July 2015, New York Magazine ran a multimedia cover story that photographed and individually interviewed 35 of the women who had encounters with Cosby, some of whom were in their teens at the time. The essays have similar details, with most of the women stating that they were drugged without their awareness or consent. Some of the interviewees also recount being directly assaulted.

"We must ask ourselves if the lesson we want to teach our kids is that, again, a woman's voice and body are not valuable or precious or valid," said model/actress Beverly Johnson to People, having also been featured in the New York Mag article. Johnson had stated in a Vanity Fair essay that Cosby had also surreptitiously drugged her during the days of The Cosby Show. "I know my truth, and I hope for a society that is sensitive to the protection of women, regardless of the stakes."

Cosby was to be deposed by Dickinson's team in relation to her defamation suit, but in late November Cosby's attorneys filed a request to have the deposition put on hold. Then in mid-December, in response to a group of seven women suing him for defamation via a Massachusetts court, Cosby filed a federal countersuit stating that said plaintiffs are making "malicious, opportunistic, and false and defamatory" charges. Days later, Cosby sued Johnson for defamation over her allegations of attempted assault.

As a result of the disturbing accusations, numerous colleges revoked honorary degrees awarded to Cosby. Additionally, a statue of the comedian was removed from Disney's MGM Hollywood Studios park in July 2015.

Arrest and Trial

Although more than 50 women came forward with claims that the legendary comedian and actor had sexually violated and/or drugged them, Cosby managed to fend off the accusations. However, on December 30, 2015, a warrant was issued for Cosby's arrest for the alleged drugging and sexual assault of Andrea Constand in January 2004, a month shy of when the statute of limitations to file legal action would have expired.

On May 24, 2016, a judge in Pennsylvania determined there was enough evidence for the sexual assault case to proceed with a criminal trial. Following pretrial hearings in December, the trial was scheduled to begin the following spring, with Cosby facing a prison sentence of up to 30 years over three counts of aggravated indecent assault.

In June 2017, Constand took the stand to testify about her relationship with Cosby and her version of events. She said she viewed the older comedian as a mentor and, as a gay woman, she had no interest in a romantic relationship. However, during the night in question, she said he provided three pills to help her relax, and then proceeded to force himself on her when she was "paralyzed" and unable to resist. The defense countered by highlighting some of the inconsistencies in her explanation, and asked why she continued to maintain contact with Cosby if her accounts of being violated were true.

Although testimonies and closing arguments were delivered within six days, it soon became clear that the jury was having difficulty reaching a verdict, as they requested to review evidence multiple times. On June 17, with the jury deadlocked on all three counts following 52 hours of deliberations, the judge declared a mistrial.

Afterward, Cosby's publicist declared the result a "total victory" and lauded his client's restored legacy. However, the prosecution team rejected that depiction of the outcome and promised to bring Cosby back to trial.

On April 26, 2018, Bill Cosby was retried and convicted of three counts of sexual assault. He may spend a maximum of 10 years in prison for each count.

RICHARD PRYOR

Richard Pryor was an African-American stand-up comedian, actor, television writer, and a social critic. A highly-acclaimed comedy star, he was as renowned for his hilarious improvisations during his live comedy shows as for his dashing lifestyle, many affairs, and a lifelong battle with drug addiction. He influenced many up and coming, modern comic artists with his flair for captivating the audience through minute observations and skillful storytelling.

Considered as one of the brightest stars of his generation, Pryor influenced generations of stand-up comedians and was referred to as 'The Picasso of our Profession', and 'The Seminal Comedian of the Last 50 Years' by his colleagues. Pryor was one of the top entertainers of the 1970s and 1980s and holds the honor of being listed at the top spot on Comedy Central's list of 'All-Time Greatest Stand-Up Comedians' and Rolling Stone Magazine's 'Fifty Best Stand-Up Comedians of All Time'. Pryor was an animal rights activist and campaigned for the protection of elephants.

Childhood & Early Life

Richard Pryor was born Richard Franklin Lennox Pryor the Third, on December 1, 1940, in Peoria, Illinois, Chicago to Gertrude L. (Thomas), and LeRoy "Buck Carter" Pryor, a former boxer and hustler who also served the military during World War II.

His mother abandoned him when he was ten years old and he was raised by his grandmother, Marie Carter, in a brothel. His upbringing was stern and unforgiving, resulting in beatings for the smallest of eccentricities.

Pryor was one of the four children raised in his grandmother's brothel and was sexually abused at age seven by a teenage neighbor and later by a childhood preacher.

Despite these circumstances, he played the part of class clown at school and discovered his acting skills in his early teens.

He was expelled from school at the age of 14and ended up working a string of jobs until he joined the military.

Pryor served in the army for only two years, as he was discharged for fighting with another soldier.

Career

After his stint in the military, Richard Pryor moved to New York City to try his luck in acting in 1963 and began performing acts in various clubs in New York.

In 1964, he made his television debut on the variety show 'On Broadway Tonight'.

He debuted on the big screen in 1967with 'The Busy Body' and followed through with 'Wild In The Streets' in 1968.Pryor's first, self-titled comedy album released in 1968 as well, which was inspired by those turbulent years of his life.

The early 1970s were majorly successful for Pryor. He released his second album 'Craps (After Hours)'. The major breakthrough came due to his role in 'Wattstax', a tragi-comic documentary.

Pryor's original content then started attracting a lot of attention. His comedy was like a breath of fresh air, despite, or perhaps because of its X-rated content. Richard's third comedy album 'That Nigger's Crazy' sold extremely well and won the 'Grammy Award for Best Comedic Recording' in 1976. The era of the late 1970ssaw him create a thriving career as an actor, with acclaimed performances in 11 films.

The first major blow his career suffered was because of his drinking, smoking, and drug habits. After this health crisis, hepicked himself up and started working on what later came to be known as his finest performance.The film 'Richard Pryor: Live in Concert'(1979) garnered a lot of praise and was sold out in many urban movie theaters.

In 1980, Richard Pryor allegedly tried to commit suicide by

pouring rum all over himself and lighting himself on fire. He was restrained by the police while running thus on the street and taken to the hospital for treatment of severe burns.

After a lengthy recovery, he returned to stand-up comedy and acting. In 1983, Pryor became one of the highest-paid African-American actors, reportedly charging $4 million to play an evil henchman in Superman III.

In the autobiographical film 'Jo Jo Dancer, Your Life is Calling' (1986), he used his own life experience to play a popular stand-up comic who takes a look at his life while recuperating in a hospital. The film was not successful.

In 1986, after being diagnosed with multiple sclerosis he did his best to remain active, starring in several movies. By theearly 1990s, he was confined to a wheelchair; still he kept performing stand-up comedy and acting. His last film appearance was in 'Lost Highway'(1997).

Major Work

Richard Pryor's first major success was his third album, 'That Nigger's Crazy', which released in 1974 and became a certified Gold hit. His next two albums, '....Is It Something I Said?' and 'Bicentennial Nigger' enjoyed similar critical and commercial success.

He starred in 12 movies during the 1970s-80s, including box office hits such as 'Lady Sings the Blues' (1972), 'Silver

Streak'(1976) with Gene Wilder, 'Blue Collar' (1978), and more.

Pryor reteamed with Gene Wilder for the popular crime comedy 'Stir Crazy'(1980); the film was a huge hit at the box office, earning more than $100 million.

The comedian wrote the autobiography 'Pryor Convictions: And Other Life Sentences' with Todd Gold, earning critical acclaim upon its release in 1995.

Awards & Achievements

He won an Emmy Award in 1973 (Best Writing in Comedy in collaboration with Lily Tomlin) for his work on 'The Lily Tomlin Show'.

He won three consecutive Grammy Awards from 1974 to 1976 and others in 1981, 1982 for 'Best Writing in Comedy'.

Pryor co-hosted the 'Academy Award' twice - in 1977, and in 1983.

He has also won two 'American Academy of Humor Awards' and 'Writers Guild of America Award' for his humor portrayed in his stand-up comedy acts.

The first-ever 'Kennedy Center Mark Twain Prize for American Humor' was presented to him in 1998.

Personal Life

Pryor married seven times to five women and fathered seven children.

His first daughter was Renee Pryor, born in 1957, when he was 17, to his then girlfriend Susan.

He married Patricia Pryor in 1960 and had a son, Richard Pryor Jr., in 1961. He divorced Patricia the following year.

His third child was Elizabeth Ann, born in April 1967 to his girlfriend, Maxie Anderson.

He then married Shelley Bonis in 1967 and divorced her in 1969. The couple had a child, Rain Pryor, born in April 1969.

On 22nd September 1977, he married Deborah McGuire and they divorced the following year.

He married Jennifer Lee in August 1981 and divorced the next year but later remarried in June 2001 and remained married until his death.

He married his fifth wife, Flynn Belaine in October 1986 and divorced the next year but later remarried in April 1990, unfortunately divorcing again in July 1991. The couple had two kids; Steven, born in 1984, and Kelsey, born in October 1987.

He also fathered a child, Franklin, born in 1987, with actress and model, Geraldine Mason.

He had relationships with actresses Pam Grier and Margot Kidder.

He died at age 65, on December 10, 2005, suffering a heart attack in Los Angeles.

FASCINATING FACTS ABOUT RICHARD PRYOR

Richard Pryor, who would have turned 76 years old today, is considered by many to be the greatest stand-up comedians of all time. Jerry Seinfeld referred to him as "the Picasso of our profession." Chris Rock has called him comedy's Rosa Parks. Yet the indelible mark Pryor made on the world of comedy only tells part of his story.

Like his career in the spotlight, Pryor's world offstage was also highly compelling and full of shocking turns. He's one of those people whose real life was so off-the-wall at times that it becomes tough to separate fact from fiction. Here are just a few stories about the brilliant and chaotic life of the great Richard Pryor.

1. HE HAD A TRAGIC CHILDHOOD

Richard Pryor had a tragic early life, experiencing things that no child should have to endure: Born to a prostitute named Gertrude on December 1, 1940 in Peoria, Illinois, Pryor's father was a notoriously violent pimp named LeRoy Pryor. For much of his childhood, Pryor was raised in the actual brothel where his mother worked, which was owned by his own no-nonsense grandmother, Marie Carter. With his mother periodically drop-ping out of his life for long stretches, it was Marie who served as Pryor's central guardian and caretaker.

In 2015, The New Yorker published an article to mark the 10th anniversary of Pryor's passing, which offered further details on his turbulent early life, noting:

Pryor said that one of the reasons he adored movies as a boy was that you were never in doubt as to why the women in them were screaming. As for the sounds that Richard heard in the middle of the night in his room on the top floor of one of Marie's businesses, he had no idea what was happening to those girls. A number of times, he saw his mother, Gertrude, one of the women in Marie's employ, nearly beaten to death by his father. Gertrude left when Richard was five. He later registered no resentment over this. "At least Gertrude didn't flush me down the toilet," he said. (This was not a joke. As a child, Pryor opened a shoebox and found a dead baby inside.)

2. HE WALKED AWAY FROM A SUCCESSFUL CAREER

Early in his career Pryor found success by modeling his comedy largely on the work on Bill Cosby, which led to many comparisons being drawn between the two—a fact that Cosby reportedly grew to dislike.

There are conflicting tales of just how Pryor made the 180-degree change in style that led to him becoming a comedic legend. One of the most well traveled tales, and one that Pryor himself confirmed on more than one occasion, states that Pryor was performing his clean-cut act in Las Vegas one night when he looked out into the audience and saw Dean Martin among the crowd. If you believe the story, seeing the legendarily cool

Rat Packer's face made Pryor question what exactly he was doing and caused him to abruptly leave the stage mid-performance. Around this time Pryor moved to the San Francisco Bay area, dropped out of the comedy limelight for several years, and later reemerged with the more pointed, in-your-face style that made him an icon.

3. HE MADE LORNE MICHAELS QUIT SATURDAY NIGHT LIVE

Back in 1975, Saturday Night Live was brand new, so at the time the show's creator, Lorne Michaels, wasn't yet a powerful TV icon. Therefore, when Michaels stuck his neck out and demanded the right to have Pryor on as a guest host, he was really risking a lot. It took Michaels handing in a fake resignation to convince NBC executives to allow the famously foulmouthed comic to appear. Michaels himself had to implement a secret five-second delay for that night's episode to be sure that any off-the-cuff, unscripted choice language didn't make its way out over the airwaves. The delay was kept from Pryor who, upon later finding out, confirmed that he would have refused to do the show had he known about it

The episode, the seventh one of SNL's premiere season, contained one of the most memorable and edgy sketches ever to appear on the show: (the NSFW) Word Association. Chevy Chase and Pryor's personal writer, Paul Mooney, have each claimed to have written the sketch.

. . .

4. HE LOST THE STARRING ROLE IN BLAZING SADDLES

Pryor and Gene Wilder made four films together (Silver Streak; Stir Crazy; See No Evil, Hear No Evil; and Another You), but there could have been at least one more. Pryor was one of the credited writers on Mel Brooks's classic Blazing Saddles and the plan for a time was that he would also co-star in the film, playing Sheriff Bart alongside Wilder as the Waco Kid. In the clip above, Wilder explained how Pryor's legendary drug use caused him to end up in a remote city and subsequently lose the starring role to Cleavon Little.

5. IT WASN'T A DRUG MISHAP THAT CAUSED PRYOR TO SET HIMSELF ON FIRE

One of the most retold stories about Pryor centers around the incident on June 9, 1980 where he set himself on fire and took off running down a Los Angeles street fully engulfed in flames. Though he wasn't expected to survive the episode, he eventually pulled through and spent the next six weeks recuperating in the hospital. At the time it was often reported that the cause of the accident was Pryor freebasing cocaine. Pryor later admitted that in a drug-fueled psychosis he had actually attempted to kill himself by dousing his body in 151-proof rum and setting himself ablaze. A friend of Pryor's at the time has gone on record as saying that the idea for the act likely came about that evening after the two of them watched footage of Thích Qu?ng Ð?c, the Vietnamese monk who famously burned himself to death in 1963 as an act of protest.

. . .

6. HE WAS A FREQUENT GROOM

Pryor was married seven times to five different women. In the 2013 documentary Omit the Logic, a friend of Pryor's—who served as the best man at one of his weddings—recounts how Pryor showed up at his hotel room door just a few hours after marrying Jennifer Lee, insisting that he already wanted a divorce. Pryor would get divorced from Lee the next year, only to remarry her 19 years later; the two were still together when Pryor passed away in 2005.

7. HE HAD A SOFT SPOT FOR ANIMALS

In 1986 Pryor was diagnosed with multiple sclerosis, a central nervous system disease that ultimately left him confined to a wheelchair. Pryor was such an avid supporter of animal rights, however, that he actively spoke out against animal testing of any kind—even when that testing meant getting closer to a cure for his own condition. The biography on RichardPryor.com provides more insight into this part of his private life:

He's been honored by PETA, the People for the Ethical Treatment of Animals, for saving baby elephants in Botswana targeted for circuses. In 2000, as the Ringling Bros. and Barnum & Bailey Circus was preparing to open at Madison Square Garden, Pryor gave the Big Top's first African-American ringmaster, Jonathan Lee Iverson, something to think about when he wrote him a letter in which he stated: "While I am hardly one to complain about a young African American making an honest living, I urge you to ask yourself just how honorable it is to preside over the abuse and suffering of animals."

8. DESPITE HIS DETERIORATING HEALTH, HE NEVER STOPPED PERFORMING

Even while MS continued to rob him of his mobility, Pryor's comedic mind continued cranking. Throughout the early 1990s Pryor would often show up at Los Angeles's famous standup club The Comedy Store to take to the stage in his wheelchair. In the above clip from The Joe Rogan Experience, a few comics discuss what it was like to watch the all-time great perform in his diminished state.

EDWARD MURPHY

Eddie Murphy is an American comedian and actor, known for his witty sense of humor and inspiring characters. He was a gifted artist since his childhood and used to perform stand-up acts in front of his friends. He was a creative and ambitious child with an amusing personality. His dream was to become a comedian and entertain the world with his clever and smart sense of humor.

He first stepped on the ladder of success when he got the role of comedian in a television show. He grabbed the opportunity with both hands and succeeded in creating a name for himself in the entertainment world and built his own fan base. It led to his first major motion picture release which was succeeded by one after another. His personal life has also been very much talked about because of his multiple relationships and his children from various women. But his real success lies in winning the hearts of people through his award winning roles and inspiring portrayal of characters in movies. He has been accepted and appreciated throughout the world by the audiences for his delightful performances.

Childhood & Early Life

He was born on April 3, 1961 in Brooklyn, New York to Lillian, a telephone operator and Charles Edward Murphy, a New York police officer and an amateur comedian.

His parents got divorced when he was three years old. When he was five, his father died and his mother became very ill. As a result, he and his elder brother, Charlie, lived in foster care for a year.

When he was nine, his mother married Vernon Lynch, a foreman at an ice cream plant and the family moved to the primarily African-American suburb of Roosevelt, Long Island.

As a kid, he used to watch a lot of television and impersonated characters such as Bugs Bunny and Bullwinkle. He was voted as the "most popular" of his graduating class because of his witty humor.

He got enrolled in Nassau Community College and worked part time as a shoe store clerk. He also used to perform at local clubs and bars.

Career

In 1981, he auditioned for a role in NBC's popular late night comedy show, 'Saturday Night Fever', and got selected. He performed periodically in the show until one night, when a few minutes of airtime was left without any content, he was asked to fill it with his stand-up performance.

His performance was delightful and he became one of the main comedians in the show thereafter. He created memorable characters such as Mister Robinson, an urban version of TV's Mister Rogers and an illiterate convict and poet named Tyrone Green.

In 1982, he got his first major movie role in '48 Hours', alongside Nick Nolte. The film was a commercial success and Murphy was highly appreciated for his charming performance in it. It was followed by his next successful movie venture 'Trading Places' in 1983.

In 1984, his performance in the movie 'Beverly Hills Cop' made him a superstar and he was nominated for a Golden Globe Award for his performance in the film.He also appeared in its sequel in 1987, 'Beverly Hills Cop II', which too was a commercial success.

His next successful movie was a romantic comedy 'Coming to America' with Arsenio Hall, in 1988. In 1990, he took a break from movies after the failure of his movie 'Another 48 Hours', a sequel to his 1982 flick '48 Hours'.

Upon his return, he did several movies which were also commercially unsuccessful. In 1996, he appeared in the comedy 'The Nutty Professor' which was a success at the box-office. He also voiced the role of donkey in the animated

'Shrek' movie franchise which became popular with the audience.

His next positively acclaimed performance was in the movie 'Dreamgirls' in 2006. After that, he appeared in movies such as 'Meet Dave' (2008), 'Imagine That' (2009) and 'Tower Heist' (2011).

Awards & Achievements

He was honored in the 'Best Actor' category by the 'National Society of Film Critics Awards' and 'Saturn Awards' for his performance in the 1996 movie 'The Nutty Professor'.

In 2007, he was nominated in the 'Best Supporting Actor' category in 'Academy Awards' and won the 'Golden Globe Award' and the 'Screen Actors Guild Award' for his performance in the movie 'Dreamgirls'.

He also received Kids Choice Award for the 'The Best Voice from an Animated Film' for his movies 'Shrek the Third' and 'Shrek Forever' in the year 2008 and 2011 respectively.

Personal Life & Legacy

He has a son with Tamara Hood, named Christian Murphy, born on November 29, 1990 and another son with Paulette McNeely named Eric Murphy, born on July 10, 1989.

He began a relationship with a lawyer, Nicole Mitchell, in 1988 and got married to her on March 18, 1993 after two years of live-in relationship. They were blessed with five children. On April 17, 2006, they got divorced after 13 years of marriage.

After his divorce, he began dating Spice Girl 'Melanie Brown', who became pregnant and gave birth to a girl on April 3, 2007 which was later confirmed to be Murphy's daughter, Angel Iris Murphy Brown.

In January 2008, he exchanged marriage vows with Tracey Edmonds, a film producer, in a private ceremony on an island. They planned on having a legal ceremony upon their return to U.S. but it never happened as they broke up after sometime when he started dating an actress, Paige Butcher.

Here are a few facts about Eddie Murphy that you all must know:

- Edward Regan Murphy, popularly known as Eddie, was born on April 3rd, 1961 in Brooklyn, NYC, USA.
- Eddie is an African/American actor, comedian, director, writer, and singer.
- Eddie's mother used to work as a telephone operator, whereas his father worked as a transit police officer. He was raised by his mother and stepdad when his father died. He was really young at that time. Unfortunately, Eddie's mother became extremely ill which made him and his brother Charlie live in a foster home for 1 year in Roosevelt, New York City.
- He started developing his comedy skills in the foster home where he used to write and perform his own written comedy skits by the young age of 15. He was

extremely influenced by Bill Cosby in his early learning days.

- Eddie Murphy married Nicole Mitchell with whom he has 5 children – Bria Murphy, Myles Mitchell, Shayne Audra, Zola Ivy and Bella Zahra. He has two more children from his previous relationships namely Christian and Eric. He also has a daughter named Angel Iris Murphy Brown from Melanie Brown, the famous 'Scary Spice' from the band, 'The Spice'
- According to the box-office, Eddie Murphy is the 4th highest grossing amazing actor in the USA.
- Eddie Murphy has proudly received Golden Globe Award nominations for his amazing performances in Beverly Hill Cop series, 48 Hrs. The Nutty Professor and Trading Places.
- Murphy has won a Golden Globe Award as the Best Supporting Actor for the movie Dream girls.
- Murphy has also worked as a voice-over artist for animated characters such as Donkey in Shrek series, Thurgood Stubbs in The PJs and Chinese dragon Mushu in the amazing Disney movie Mulan.
- The motto of Eddie Murphy's life is to believe in clean and healthy living that's why he doesn't drink alcohol or smoke.

ROBERT TOWNSEND

Robert Townsend is an American actor, film director, and writer. He is popular for his commercially successful movies such as Hollywood Shuffle, Eddie Murphy's "Raw", and The Meteor Man.

Early life, childhood, and education:

He was born on February 6, 1957, in Chicago, United States. His parents were Shirley and Ed Townsend. However, he grew up with his three siblings by his mother as a single parent. From a very young age, he was amazed at the television. Spending his time watching and studying it, he began to practice by impersonating famous characters. He was a versatile actor from a very young age.

.   .   .

Personal life

Talking about his personal life, Robert married Cheri Jones on September 15, 1990, after they knew each other. After their marriage, they gave birth to two beautiful daughters, Sierra and Skylar (Skye Townsend), and a son, Isiah. Interestingly, both of his daughters followed his footsteps by starting their career as entertainers. Despite having a great family, Robert and Cheri decided to end their relationship by getting a divorce on August 9, 2001. Since then, not much is known about his relationships. It seems that he is focusing more on his career as an actor rather than letting out details about his personal life. Given his age, it evident that he has been married but the details are waiting to be found out. Due to an absence of much information, his fans are continually curious to discover more about him.

Career and accomplishments

As a versatile actor, his talent caught the attention of Chicago's Experimental Bag Theatre. Robert sparkled in his hometown of Chicago, where he went to New York's famous comedy club the Improvisation. His debut in traditional urban classic, Cooley High (1975). His break came while starring on television comedy specials, Rodney Dangerfield: It's Not Easy Bein' Me (1986) and Uptown Comedy Express (1987). Later on, he wrote, directed, produced and starred in his first film, Hollywood Shuffle (1987). Later on, he landed roles on various successful movies such as Eddie Murphi Raw (1987), The Five Heartbeats (1991), The Meteor Man (1993), Partners in Crime

(2005). He created and starred in the WB Network's sitcom The Parent 'Hood (1995). As of now, he has a net worth of $2 Million.

Comedy Career

Worked with Experimental Black Actors Guild and Second City, Chicago, mid-1970s; worked with Negro Ensemble Company, acted in Off-Broadway productions, and performed at local comedy clubs, New York City, late 1970s-early 1980s; film appearances include Cooley High, American International, 1975; Streets of Fire, Universal, 1984; A Soldier's Story, Columbia, 1984; American Flyers, Warner Bros., 1985; Odd Jobs, 1985; Ratboy, Warner Bros., 1986; Hollywood Shuffle, Samuel Goldwyn Co., 1987; The Mighty Quinn, MGM/UA, 1989; That's Adequate, South Gate Entertainment, 1990; and The Five Heartbeats, Twentieth Century Fox, 1991; participated in comedic features It's Not Easy Bein' Me, 1987, and Uptown Comedy Express, 1989. Co-wrote, directed, and produced Hollywood Shuffle and The Five Heartbeats ; directed Raw, Paramount, 1987, and Partners in Crime, HBO, 1987-88.

Film Career

After high school, Townsend enrolled at Illinois State University, studied a year and later moved to New York to study at the Negro Ensemble Company. Townsend's mother believed that he should complete his college education, but he felt that college took time away from his passion for acting, and he soon dropped out of school to pursue his acting career full-time. Townsend auditioned to be part of Saturday Night Live's' 1980–1981 cast, but was rejected in favor of Eddie Murphy. In 1982, Townsend appeared as one of the main characters in the PBS series Another Page, a program produced by Kentucky Educational Television that taught literacy to adults through serialized stories. Townsend later appeared in small parts in films like A Soldier's Story (1984), directed by Norman Jewison, and after its success garnered much more substantial parts in films like The Mighty Quinn (1989) with Denzel Washington.[6]In 1987, Townsend wrote, directed and produced Hollywood Shuffle, a satire based on the hardships and obstacles that black actors undergo in film industry. The success of his first project helped him establish credit in the industry. One of his films was the musical The Five Heartbeats based on 1960s R&B male groups and the tribulations of the music industry. Townsend created and produced two television variety shows—the CableACE award–winning Robert Townsend and His Partners in Crime for HBO, and the Fox Television variety show Townsend Television (1993). Townsend also created and starred in the WB Network's sitcom The Parent 'Hood with originally ran from January 1995 to July 1999. Townsend was Programming Director at the Black Family Channel, but the network folded in 2007. Townsend created The Robert Townsend Foundation, a non-profit organization whose mission is to introduce and help new unsigned filmmakers.

BERNIE MAC

Bernie Mac was born on October 5, 1957, in Chicago, Illinois. His first standup routine was at the age of eight for his church congregation. He established a variety show at Chicago's Regal Theatre, made appearances on HBO's "Def Comedy Jam" and joined the cast of "Ocean's Eleven." On August 9, 2008, Mac died of pneumonia.

Acting Debut

Mac's acting career started with a role as a club doorman in the comedy Mo' Money (1992) and also appeared as Pastor Clever in Friday (1995). Mac's frequent appearances on HBO's Def Comedy Jam in the early 1990s also helped put him on the map.

Mac's edgy comedy seemed an unlikely fit for television, but after frequent appearances on the series Moesha and gaining wide acclaim for his starring role in Spike Lee's The Original

Kings of Comedy in 2000, Mac was primed to create a sitcom on his own terms.

Early Life

Mac performed his first standup routine at the age of eight, impersonating his grandparents at the dinner table for the church congregation.

After losing his mother to cancer (his brother, father and grand-mother died not long after), Mac realized the healing power of laughter. He began telling jokes for spare change in the Chicago subway. While working various odd jobs, he eventually established his own weekly variety show at Chicago's Regal Theatre and joined the comedy club circuit in 1977.

Career

Bernie Mac's life changed completely after he participated in the 'Miller Lite Comedy Search' contest and won it. He gained a lot of popularity after doing a famous stand-up comedy act on 'Def Comedy Jam', a television series produced by the channel 'HBO'.

He later appeared in stand-up comedy shows that featured comedians like Dionne Warwick, Redd Foxx and Natalie Cole.

After a couple of blink-and-miss roles in movies like 'Mo' Money' and 'Who's The Man?', Bernie Mac was offered the character of Uncle Vester in the comedy flick 'House Party 3', which released in 1994. He was also seen in the movie 'Above The Rim' in the same year.

1995 saw the release of his two other flicks, namely 'The Walking Dead' and 'Friday'. While 'Friday', a comic flick, was a success, 'The Walking Dead' failed miserably.

During the period 1996-99, Bernie Mac appeared in various films, such as 'How To Be A Player', 'Booty Call', 'B*A*P*S' and 'The Players Club'. His most noteworthy performance during this period was his portrayal of Bundini Brown in the flick 'Don King: Only In America'.

In 2001, Bernie Mac was seen in the Hollywood blockbuster 'Ocean's Eleven', where he shared the screen with stalwarts like Brad Pitt and George Clooney.

In 2003, he was seen in three big budget movies, namely 'Head of State', 'Charlie's Angels: Full Throttle' and 'Bad Santa'. All the three movies were commercially successful ventures.

In 2004, he was seen in two important films, namely 'Mr. 3000' and 'Ocean's Twelve' – the sequel to the 2001 film.

Bernie Mac reprised his role of Frank Catton in the third instalment of the Ocean's franchise titled 'Ocean's Thirteen', which released in 2007.

He played the characters Zuba and Floyd Henderson in the movird 'Madagascar: Escape 2 Africa' and 'Soul Men' respectively. Both these movies were released in 2008.

The last film of his illustrious career was 'Old Dogs', in which he had essayed the character Jimmy Lunchbox. The ensemble of this 2009 film included several renowned names like John Travolta, Robin Williams and Kelly Preston. He also played a cameo in the Hollywood blockbuster 'Transformers' which released the same year.

Major Works

Bernie Mac is best known for his sitcom called 'The Bernie Mac Show'. The episodes of the television show were mostly hilarious takes on the events which took place in his life. The show was a big hit with the American television viewers and catapulted Bernie Mac to the league of best comedians in the nation. The show ran for five years, from 2001 to 2006

Awards & Achievements:

In 2002-03, Bernie Mac was nominated for two 'Emmy Awards' for his role in the television show 'The Bernie Mac Show'. He also won a 'Television Critics Association Award' during the same time for his impeccable acting in the same show.

In 2003, he bagged a 'Prism Award' as well as a 'Satellite Award' for his performance in 'The Bernie Mac Show'.

During the period 2003-07, Bernie Mac was felicitated with the 'NAACP Image Award' in the 'Outstanding Actor In A Comedy Series' category 4 times, for his role in the TV show 'The Bernie Mac Show'.

. . .

Personal Life

Besides his work in film and television Mac also authored two books, 2001's I Ain't Scared of You: Bernie Mac on How Life Is and his 2003 memoir, Maybe You Never Cry Again. The latter described Mac's impoverished childhood, strict upbringing and his mother's belief in him.

In 1977 at age 19, Mac married his high school sweetheart, Rhonda, whom he credits with much of his success, particularly as the young couple struggled through the early years of Mac's fledgling career. They had a daughter, Je'Niece, and a grand-daughter.

On August 9, 2008, Mac died of pneumonia. More than 6,000 people attended a memorial service for Mac at the House of Hope Church on Chicago's South Side

He suffered from Sarcoidosis, an ailment which causes inflammation in tissues. He died of cardiac arrest on 9 August 2008 at Northwestern Memorial Hospital, in Chicago, Illinois.

AFTERWORD

The decades of the 1950s and 1960s saw the rise of comics such as Don Rickles, Johnny Carson and Phyllis Diller. As the country began breaking down the walls of racism, several notable black comedians began to make audiences laugh. They were Bill Cosby and Redd Foxx. As the racial bounds were being pushed, the bounds of acceptable humor began to test the limits. Most notably, the comedy of Lenny Bruce set off what some say is the beginning of an anything subject goes style of comedy. He pushed the envelope so far that he was arrested several times for things that he said on stage. It is at this point that comedians tried to push boundaries to see just how far they could go with their comedy.

Another important development for standup comedy began in the 1950s and 1960s - television. With the advent of the television, comedians could have the best of both worlds: the physical type of comedy found in Vaudeville and also the spoken word. This saw the development of variety shows such as The Tonight Show and the Ed Sullivan show on television.

The 1970s were big for standup comedians! This is when they became superstars. They moved from being seen on television and in small comedy clubs to selling out large arenas. Comedians such as George Carlin, Cheech and Chong and Richard Pryor thrived in the new settings. In addition to their live appearances, they made recordings of their shows and sold them (as LPs) to the public. And of course the topics covered were constantly pushing the boundaries of what society would accept. As the sexual revolution and anything goes mentality became prevalent in society, the comedic topics did also.

The 1980s, 1990s and 2000s mainly followed the patterns in the previous decades, more exposure and pushing the envelope. There were however a few notable developments from these decades. MTV and Comedy Central made comedy more accessible to more people. Not only were the public getting to see the big name comics, they were being exposed to up and coming comics via the new television networks. A recent phenomenon is a comedy based reality show called "Last Comic Standing". This show gives the television viewers exposure to more inexperienced comics that could one day make it to the big leagues.

There is no telling where standup comedy will take us in the future. If the past is any indication, there will be more access by the public to standup comedians and they will always be looking for a way to make them squirm by pushing the limits of what is acceptable in society.

ACKNOWLEDGMENTS

Thank you for making us laugh in times of difficulty and bringing our families and friends together on many occasions.

Made in United States
North Haven, CT
15 April 2022

18290754R00046